A JUST FOR A DAY BOOK

WHITE BEAR, ICE BEAR

JOANNE RYDER

ILLUSTRATED BY
MICHAEL ROTHMAN

MORROW JUNIOR BOOKS / NEW YORK

For Edite, with love
J.R.

In memory of my grandparents, Nathan and Rose Smole
M.R.

Printed in the United States of America.
1 2 3 4 5 6 7 8 9 10
Library of Congress Cataloging-in-Publication Data
Ryder, Joanne.
White bear, ice bear / Joanne Ryder ; illustrated by Michael Rothman.
p.   cm.
Summary: Describes the awakening, feeding, and wandering of a
polar bear, from its own viewpoint.
ISBN 0-688-07174-0.   ISBN 0-688-07175-9 (lib. bdg.)
1. Polar bear—Juvenile literature.   [1. Polar bear.   2. Bears.]
I. Rothman, Michael, ill.   II. Title.
QL737.C27R92 1989
599.74'446—dc19   87-36781   CIP   AC

One winter morning
your room is light
and bright
            —snow white!
Outside your window
snow is falling,
calling you, changing you...

till you feel yourself
growing larger and larger.
Warm white fur covers you
—all over.

Your large furry head
touches the ceiling.
This room is too small,
too hot for you now.

So you run...outside!

Outside, everything is changed.
You are changed, too.
You are an ice bear now.

You live at the top of the world
where all winter long
the sun sleeps,
hiding beyond the ice-covered sea.

But the moon shines
in the dark winter sky,
shining its silver light
so you can see
the white snow,
the icy cliffs
all around you.

You are a white bear
walking across a white frozen sea.
Below you, sleek seals
swim in the cold dark waters.

You are a white bear
in a shadowy white world.
It is hard to see you
moving slowly across the snow.
Only your small black eyes,
your big black nose
give you away.

The air is cold and good!
You feel like running
in the cold fresh air.
Your huge furry feet,
your sharp claws
grip the rough ice.
Run, ice bear, run fast.

You are quick and curious,
climbing icy peaks
to sniff the cold air
and see others moving slowly
like pale ghosts
across the ice.

Small white foxes
watch you
from a distance.
This is their home, too.

When the wind begins to blow,
you rest as an ice bear rests,
hiding from the cold, cold wind.
You listen to the ice
creaking and groaning
as the roaring wind
blows snow
around you, over you.

When the wind stops blowing,
you get up,
stretching your long neck,
and yawn.
Your mouth opens wide,
full of sharp teeth
and a long dark tongue.
And you shake the soft snow
from your thick shaggy fur.

When you are hungry,
you hunt as an ice bear hunts,
finding a hole in the ice.
You smell a strong spicy scent.
This is a seal's place,
a seal's breathing hole.
You wait as a hunter waits,
quiet and still.

Underwater, a seal swims closer.
She needs to breathe
the cold good air above.
You see small bubbles rising—
seal's breath in the water—
as she swims up and up.
She is almost close enough
for you to catch her when...
quickly, she darts away
to another hole,
to a safer place to breathe.

You are an ice bear
wandering alone
across the icy sea.
Far above you, the dark sky
shimmers with moving lights.
Ribbons of lights,
streamers of lights
ripple and glow and dance.
You are an ice bear
and your night lights swirl
across the winter sky.

Hmmmmm.
Ever curious,
you stand up tall
and sniff the cold air
for messages, for a scent
of something familiar.
Ahhhhh! Ah, there!

You run and run.
Good supper smells call you
till you peek through a window
at another world waiting.
You leap,
ready and curious,
pushing open the door
with your large furry head
and feel warmth
changing you...

And you run inside,
hungry and happy,
home again.